With The Beatles
The historic photographs of Dezo Hoffmann

EDITED AND DESIGNED BY PEARCE MARCHBANK

THE CAPTIONS IN THIS BOOK ARE TAKEN FROM
AN INTERVIEW WITH DEZO HOFFMANN, JULY 1982.

EDITORIAL ASSISTANT: SALLY PAYNE.
PICTURE RESEARCH ASSISTANTS: HEATHER PAGE, SUE TRITTON.
LAYOUT: ALISON FENTON, MIKE BELL.
ARTWORK: HAZEL BENNINGTON, HILARY SABINE, PHIL LEVENE.
PHOTO PRINTING: REX FEATURES, DEZO HOFFMANN.
TYPESETTING: LAURA BECK TYPOGRAPHY, FOCUS PHOTOSETTING.
PRINT PRODUCTION: ROBERT SAMPSON.
PRINTED IN JAPAN BY DAI NIPPON PRINTING COMPANY, TOKYO.

BOOK © 1982 OMNIBUS PRESS (A DIVISION OF BOOK SALES LIMITED).
PHOTOGRAPHS AND CAPTIONS © DEZO HOFFMANN.
INTRODUCTION © PEARCE MARCHBANK.

ISBN 0-399-41009-0

EXCLUSIVE DISTRIBUTORS:
BOOK SALES LIMITED,
78 NEWMAN STREET, LONDON W1P 3LA, ENGLAND.
THE PUTNAM PUBLISHING GROUP,
200 MADISON AVENUE, NEW YORK, NY 10016, USA.
OMNIBUS PRESS,
GPO BOX 3304, SYDNEY, NSW 2001, AUSTRALIA.
TO THE MUSIC TRADE ONLY:
MUSIC SALES LIMITED,
78 NEWMAN STREET, LONDON W1P 3LA, ENGLAND.
MUSIC SALES CORPORATION,
799 BROADWAY, NEW YORK, NY 10003, USA.

Omnibus Press
DELILAH/PUTNAM
DISTRIBUTED BY
THE PUTNAM PUBLISHING GROUP
NEW YORK

THE FIRST MANIFESTATION OF BEATLEMANIA. OUTSIDE THE LIVERPOOL EMPIRE, MARCH 24, 1963.

In 1962 Dezo Hoffmann went to Liverpool and took his first pictures of a "smart but rather subdued" group of four young men. He had received a letter from a fan sent to *Record Mirror,* of which Dezo was staff photographer, bitterly complaining that the press was ignoring a "fab" group in Liverpool called The Beatles. He spent three days with them and this session resulted in Dezo Hoffmann catching their unique style and energy on film for the first time, and resulted in a friendship that lasted throughout the years of Beatlemania. This book shows a selection from the pictures taken by Dezo, both in public and in private, with The Beatles.

He took more shots of the group, and was closer to them, than any other photographer. He covered every major event in their career, often being the only photographer present ... their audition at Abbey Road with George Martin, their first tours of Europe and America, making their first albums, radio shows and films.

Dezo Hoffmann began work in his home country Czechoslovakia as clapper boy in the A-B Studios in

A SHOT SET-UP BY DEZO HOFFMANN TO SHOW THE WORLD-WIDE USE MADE OF HIS PICTURES ON BEATLES MERCHANDISING.

Prague, making *Eroticon* starring Hedi Lamarr. After national service in the army he joined Twentieth Century Fox in Paris and was sent to cover Mussolini's invasion of Abyssinia. Next came the Olympiad Popular in Barcelona, held by the nations boycotting Hitler's 1936 Olympics. Here he witnessed the outbreak of the Spanish Civil War. Joining the International Brigade Press Corps, he was the first newsreel man to send out footage, working alongside men such as Robert Capa and Ernest Hemingway. He was seriously wounded while filming, but followed the retreat to France. With the Second World War mobilisation he joined the Czech army, eventually arriving in England in 1940. He covered nearly all theatres of war as a news cameraman. All his war work has now been donated to the Imperial War Museum, London.

With the end of the War he joined the Crown Film Unit for a while but, as he says, "there was no excitement any more, so I deserted film-making and started in Fleet Street as a freelance photographer, being my own

boss as I was used to.'' He began to specialize in show-biz celebrities ... Charlie Chaplin, Marilyn Monroe, Louis Armstrong, Frank Sinatra, Marlene Dietrich. In 1955 he joined the weekly music paper *Record Mirror*. He applied the techniques learnt on the battle field to photographing shows and concerts, TV spectaculars and pantomime. He almost always used available light, and small format cameras. His rivals were still working with flashbulbs and cumbersome old plate cameras. He was also amongst the first to use colour film for live show-biz photography. Dezo Hoffmann is very much the Cartier Bresson of the entertainment world. He shuns publicity but at the same time gets very close to the thousands of stars he has photographed, creating everything from the most formal portrait to the most spontaneous behind-the-scenes composition.

In his thirty years of work he has built up a library of over a million negatives. A source of many extensive pictorial biographies. Many of these pictures have become archetypal images, many more have never even

been printed, let alone published. This applies to his vast collection of Beatle pictures. This book can only scratch the surface of what must be one of the most unique photo archives in pop music history, containing as it does many frames taken by the group themselves, even an 8mm colour movie, which must be the first ever film taken of them, also featuring many scenes actually shot by The Beatles.

The Beatles looked up to Dezo in the group's formative years. They were new to the business, but he was on speaking terms with so many of the stars they admired. They respected his advice and it was he, as much as anyone, who helped evolve their unique image. He knew the first day he met them that they had something vital and he wanted to show it to the world ... "to me, a London photographer who knew all the best-known groups very well, I was struck by their sincerity and simplicity". This, Dezo Hoffmann captured in images which have become part of the visual language of the twentieth century. PEARCE MARCHBANK.

FIRST RECORDING SESSION, SEPTEMBER 4, 1962, AT ABBEY ROAD:
This is the first time they worked with George Martin. They were spellbound by his musicianship. Before, they just sounded like The Shadows or anybody.'

'Ringo's own drum kit from his previous group was brought down from Liverpool. It had been George Martin's suggestion to get a new drummer.'

'Ringo has only been in the group for 18 days, and these were the first professional press pictures to be released. I put all those instruments in the foreground to camouflage George's black eye. There'd been a fight in Liverpool about Pete Best's replacement by Ringo.'

'The old Beatles Vox amplifier which they bought in Liverpool. We called their hair really long then.'

LIVERPOOL APRIL, 1963:
'This was a Record Mirror assignment. A girl had sent a picture to the paper of four young boys with long hair, complaining that we never did features on Liverpool bands. So I went up to Liverpool and they knocked me for seven. They were so fresh, so full of vitality and fun and so honest. When they found out I'd been taking pop pictures since 1953 I became a sort of father confessor to them, and would advise them on how other bands behaved, which they took advantage of. We had a genuine friendship and that's why I stayed with them.'

'This was Paul's father's house. My meeting with them was very special to them and so they dressed smart for me. We planned some little domestic scenes in the house and the garden.'

'After the house session, Paul drove us all out to Sefton Park in Liverpool. He thought he was the King of Siam in that Mark I Cortina. My bag was full of camera equipment and when they saw the cine camera and how easy it was to handle, they started to shoot. This was the first ever film of The Beatles, and shot by The Beatles themselves.'

'This is the famous 'jump' which later became the "Twist And Shout" cover. I wanted to somehow portray the vitality of those boys and I felt these pictures did just that.'

THE CAVERN APRIL, 1963:
'Taken the same day at the Cavern. Although The Beatles were never to play the Cavern again, I felt some pictures there would be useful. I wanted a working shot to capture the wine cellar atmosphere. The smell of alcohol and sweat was ridiculous down there because there was no ventilation.'

'Later Paul and I went to "Mr. Smiths" Nightclub in Manchester. Paul was dying to meet Frankie Howerd so I introduced them, even though Frankie had never heard of The Beatles. The rest of the boys were sorry they hadn't come with us when they heard.'

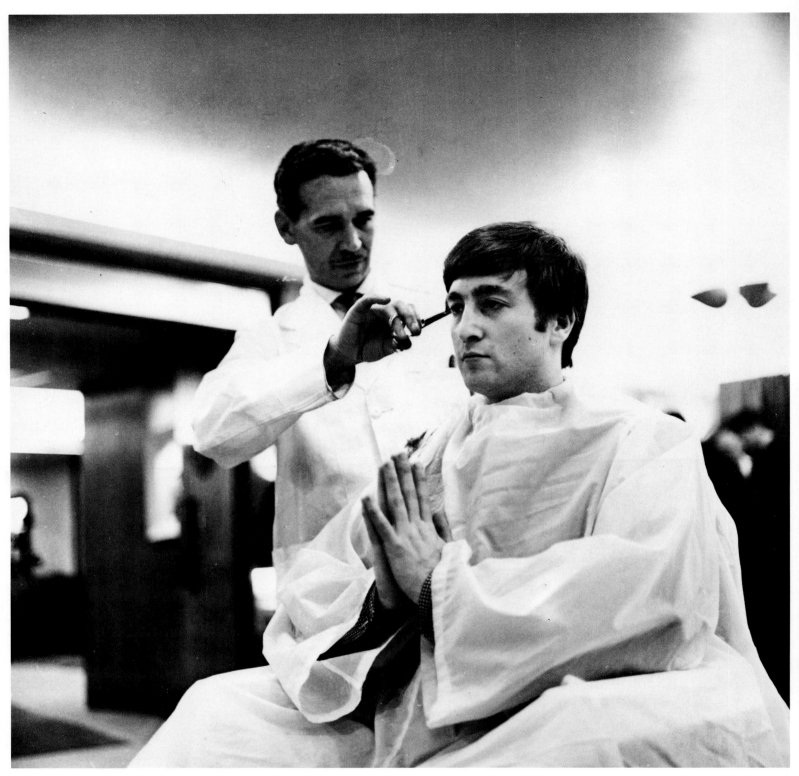

HORNES OUTFITTERS LIVERPOOL
APRIL, 1963:
'*The hairdresser was a friend of theirs who liked Astrid Kirchherr's idea of longer hair for The Beatles. He would groom and discipline their hair for them every week.*'

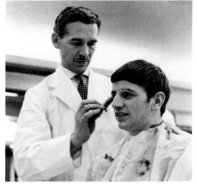

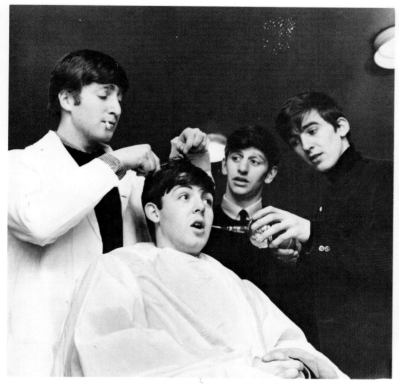
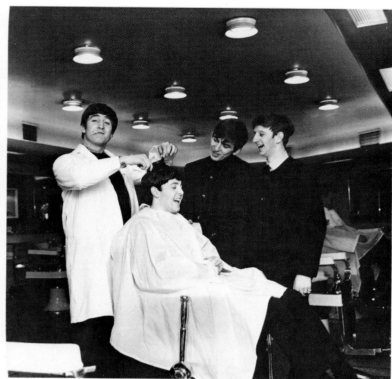
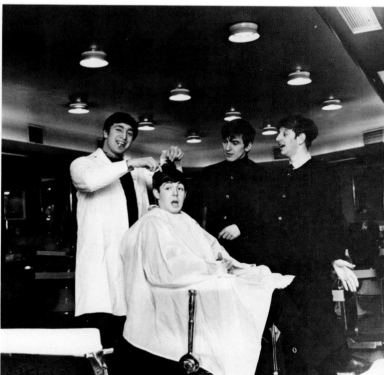

'This was a typical Beatles publicity shot. These scenes were my idea because they had no photographic ideas themselves in those days, although they were very photogenic.'

THE EMPIRE LIVERPOOL
24 MARCH, 1963:
'Their first big concert. They
were supposed to be supporting
Tommy Roe and Chris Montez
but by public demand The
Beatles were forced to close the
show and all the posters in
Liverpool had to be changed at
the last moment. It was the first
time Beatlemania really showed
itself on their home territory. I
was deafened by the sound of
screaming, clapping, and
shouting. And outside the
theatre there were millions of
people, stretching right round to
the station. It was the first time
I'd ever experienced anything
like it.'

'One of the dressing rooms was
packed with presents like this
from their fans.'

EMI MANCHESTER SQUARE, LONDON. A SILVER DISC PRESENTATION FOR ALBUM SALES OF PLEASE PLEASE ME, 22 MARCH, 1963:

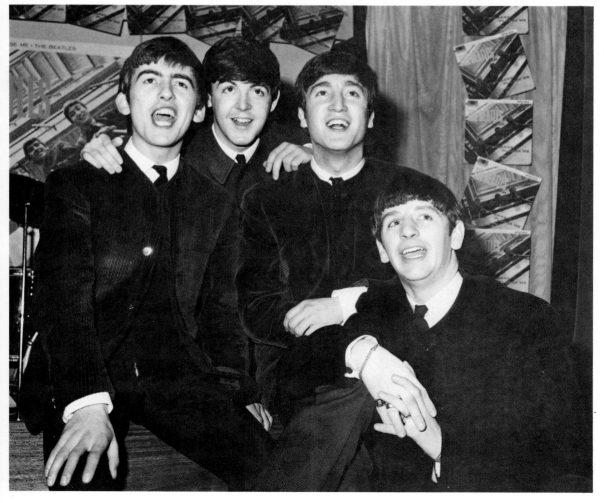

CONCERT AT STOWE SCHOOL APRIL, 1963:

'They'd never even seen an English public school before, but after the initial disappointment at it being boys only, they were pleasantly surprised. They realised it was a lot of baloney about public schoolboys being snobs, and talked with the Stowe boys as if they'd always mixed with people like that. It was a change for them after playing to decadent youths in Hamburg nightclubs and they loved it.'

'After the concert they had dinner with the headmaster and his children, and signed autographs for the boys. All the boys were beginning to grow their hair Beatle-style by then, although the craze had only been going a few months.'

'There was no screaming and the audience stayed seated throughout, which was a shock to them. But for the first time they could hear themselves play and they really let go — they would have played on for hours, they were enjoying it so much.'

'These pictures were an idea to portray them as civilised human beings, because there was a terrible anti-Beatle feeling from adults who felt they were a bad influence on their children.'

'At first neither John nor I liked this picture because it was contradictory to his tidy image. But his expression and the lighting were so good that we ended up liking it. It seems to sum up John at that time.'

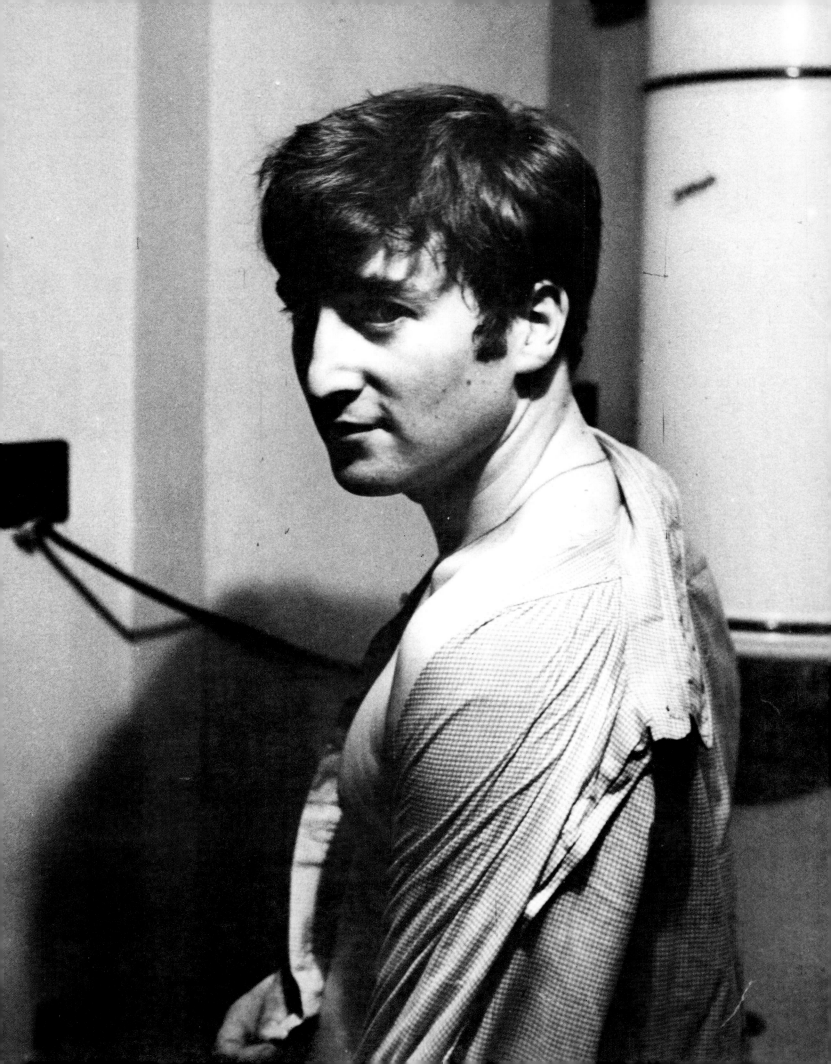

ABBEY ROAD 11 FEBRUARY, 1963:
'George Martin's main interest
was that live, they should sound
exactly like their records. He
wouldn't leave them alone for a
second, not even in the canteen.
Once he'd heard the rough
version of each song he'd go
away, work on it musically, and
come in the next day knowing
exactly what he wanted. Being
intelligent, The Beatles would
do exactly that. They never
argued musically, but about
disciplining themselves to get to
the studio on time. Sometimes
one song would be recorded 50
times and then George Martin
and Glyn Johns, the engineer,
would cut it together, staying
late into the night.'

22

'This picture was originally
going to be the cover for "Please
Please Me" but it didn't work
out.'

BBC Light Programme — "Sounds 63" broadcast live from the Albert Hall April, 1963:
'The only time The Beatles played the Albert Hall, on a bill of stars including Del Shannon, Susan Maughan, Shane Fenton.'

WESTMINSTER CAMERAS, OLD
COMPTON STREET, LONDON.
APRIL, 1963:
'This was the first time they
saw the 8mm movie we'd made
in Liverpool. They were each
given a camera by the shop in
gratitude for their advertising it.
John refused to let me use this
picture because he had his
glasses on and so we did the
whole session again.'

DEZO HOFFMANN'S STUDIO IN WARDOUR STREET, JUNE 1963:
'This was a photographic session showing The Beatles in formal studio poses. Up to this time all their photos had been more candid. I published a book, "The Beatles" and used some of these pictures. Soon afterwards, I was visited by the CID who had been contacted by the BBC. Apparently the serial numbers on the lights corresponded with those on some they'd had stolen years before. I'd bought the studio complete with fixtures and fittings, and so had to go out and get a new set of lights.'

'These were all self-portraits in
the dressing room mirror. I tried
to teach them photography
without flash, and these were a
little shaky and out-of-focus.'

'Paul and Jane Asher had only
known each other a few months,
but she helped them a lot to
adjust to London.'

BRIAN EPSTEIN, JULY 1963:
'Brian wanted his own press pictures that he could autograph for the fans. I took them against my better judgement. After all, he was their manager, not one of the group and I reckoned the worst thing he could do was compete with them. But he insisted.'

BBC MAIDA VALE, RECORDING "POP
GO THE BEATLES",
18 JUNE, 1963:
*A rare shot of Paul playing
around on the drums.*

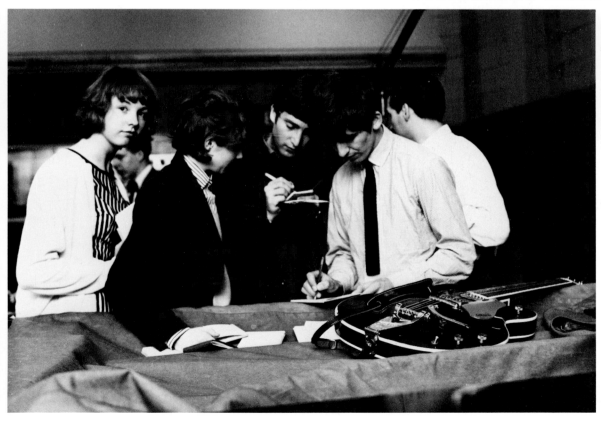

'The canteen at Maida Vale. I never went for anything arty with them. This is the sort of image I wanted to project, and I slogged at it.'

'It was Paul's 21st birthday and all they could afford for him was the bumps outside the studios in the road.'

CONTACTS (FOLLOWING 8 PAGES)
'I decided that they should and could get established individually, and so did the first split photo session. From then on, we did a lot of single pictures, and other groups started doing it too. A crowd of about 200 girls kept a solid vigil outside all through the session.'

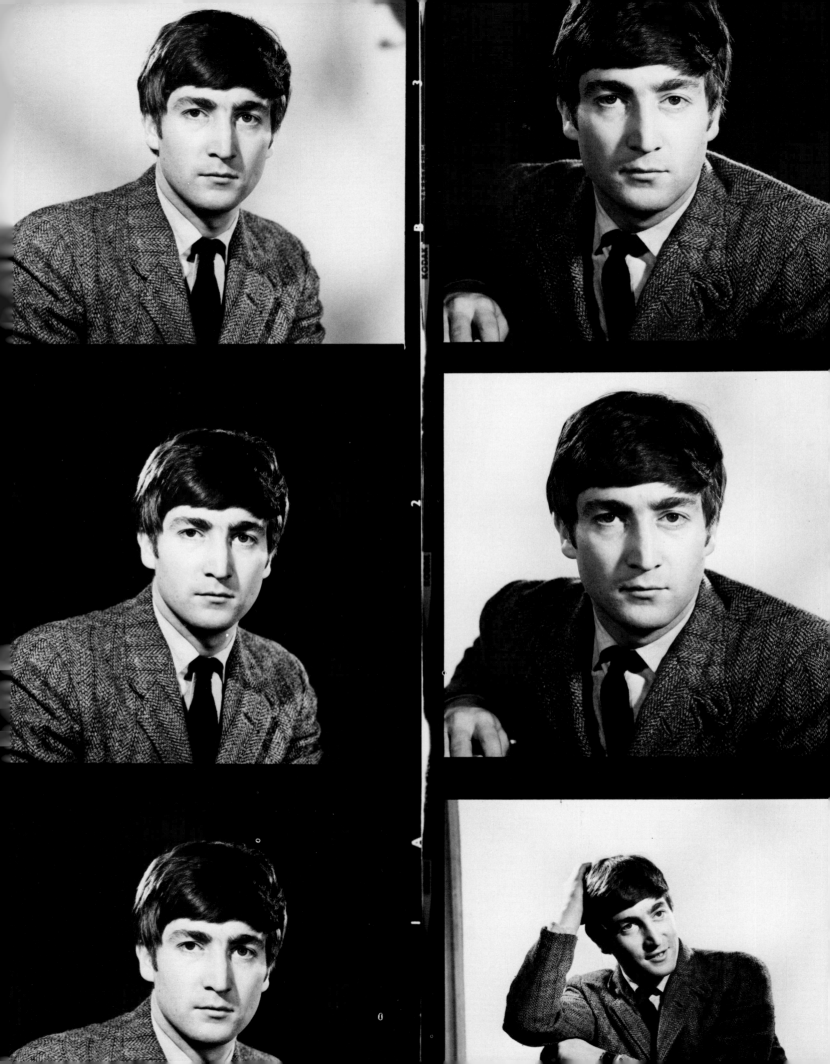

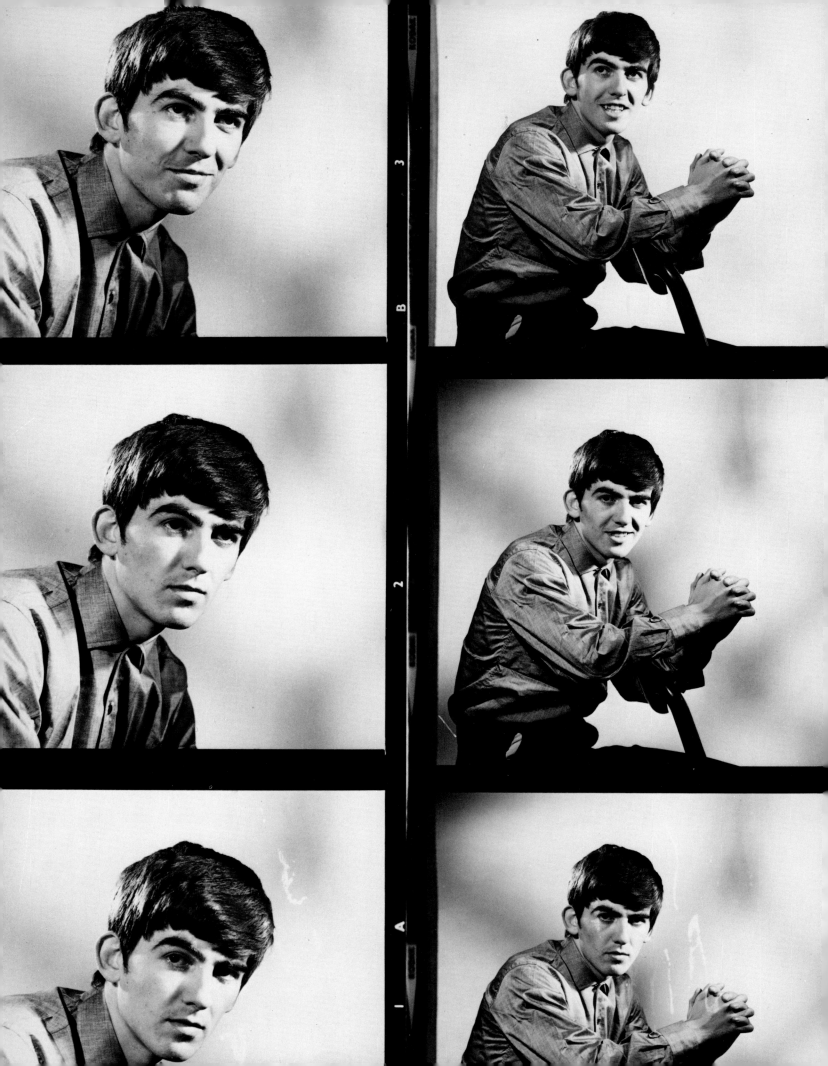

RECORDING "EASYBEAT" AT THE
PLAYHOUSE, 23 JUNE, 1963:
*'This was the first time Ringo
used his famous Ludwig kit in
public. There was only one mike
for the drums.'*

BBC PARIS CINEMA — RECORDING FOR A MIDDAY LIVE RADIO SHOW, JULY, 1963:

'These were gimmicky pictures with Liverpool comedian Ken Dodd for my benefit. They also met Wilfred Brambell there, who was later to appear with The Beatles in "A Hard Day's Night".'

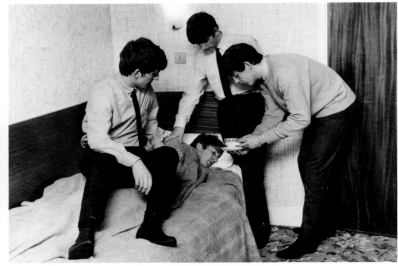

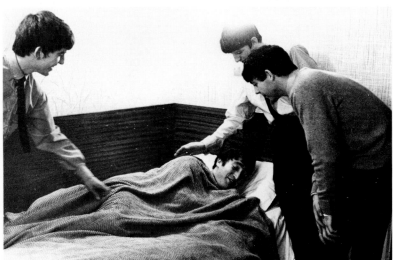

"A Day In The Life", shot in
London as a photofeature for
the Liverpool Echo, July 1963:

46

'This was their shirtmaker. I introduced them to him, he was an old Hungarian friend. This was the first time they'd had tailored clothes. They loved it.'

'I took this to capture the sordidness of Soho, because it reminded me very much of Liverpool.'

Weston-Super-Mare, 22-27 July 1963: The English tour with Gerry And The Pacemakers and Tommy Quickly:
'They filmed a lot during this session and I believe Richard Lester was inspired by this film when he directed "A Hard Day's Night".'

'The Beatles' van that carried them and all their equipment from concert to concert.'

'This session was for the American market, which as yet I hadn't been able to penetrate because the Americans didn't want to know about English pop groups. I knew I needed something strong, and since they were on a seaside tour I had the idea of hiring bathing huts, old-fashioned swimming costumes etc. They loved dressing up in silly costumes, John kept his on back at the hotel long after the session was over. The value of those pictures became huge overnight. The Daily Mirror used one as a centre spread, and America went barmy. Everybody in America used those pictures, even though they had barely heard any Beatle records. Over here, Reveille magazine used one of them as a free poster to boost their circulation figures, and it was then I realised I should do a Beatles book, and that I hadn't been wasting my time.'

'We finished the beach session, and it had been so successful that we just wanted to do more. So on the way back we stopped at this go-kart track.'

'These pictures were taken as an advertisement for Ty-Phoo Tea. Each Beatle had to shape a different letter for Ty-Phoo. We had to do it over and over until they got it right.'

FILMING A GRANADA TV SHOW IN
MANCHESTER, NOVEMBER, 1963:
*'Back on their own territory, we
could hardly get the session done
without them being mobbed.
Beatlemania had really started.'*

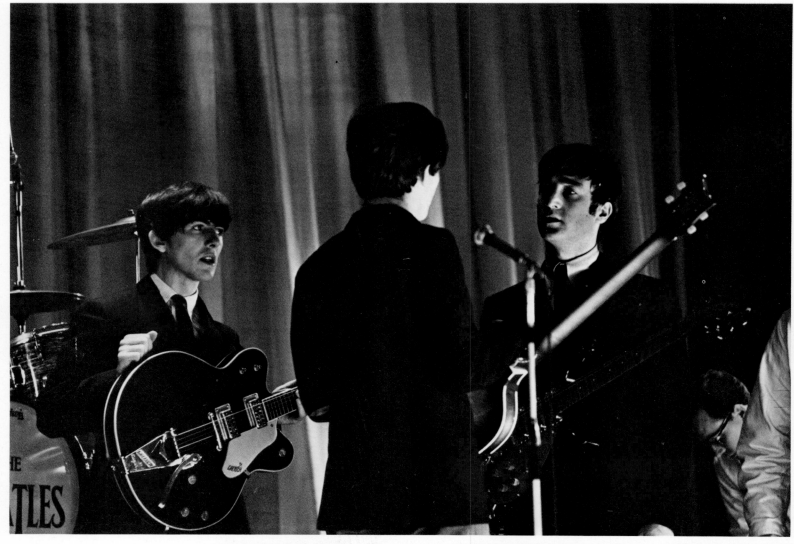

THE ROYAL VARIETY SHOW,
LONDON PALLADIUM,
4 NOVEMBER, 1963:
'The dress rehearsal for the
concert that was used by the
government to take the spotlight
off Whitehall. The Profumo
affair had just broken in the
press, and the government
squashed publicity by creating
Beatlemania. The press reported
hoards of screaming girls
besieging the Palladium,
whereas in fact there were only
about six girls there.'

'There were so many
photographers at the photo call,
which I thought was important
for them, so I made them
recreate the famous jump on the
tiny stage.'

'I used to photograph Marlene
Dietrich years before and, to me,
she had then the same innocent
spirit of The Beatles, so I
struggled to get a picture of
them together.'

On the train to Liverpool for "Juke Box Jury", BBC TV show, 11 December, 1963:

'Neil Aspinall is with them here, he was their road manager, and was closer to them than Epstein. They had a verbal understanding that the unit consisted of the four Beatles and Neil — and nobody could upset that unit. It was the first time Juke Box Jury went out from anywhere but London.'

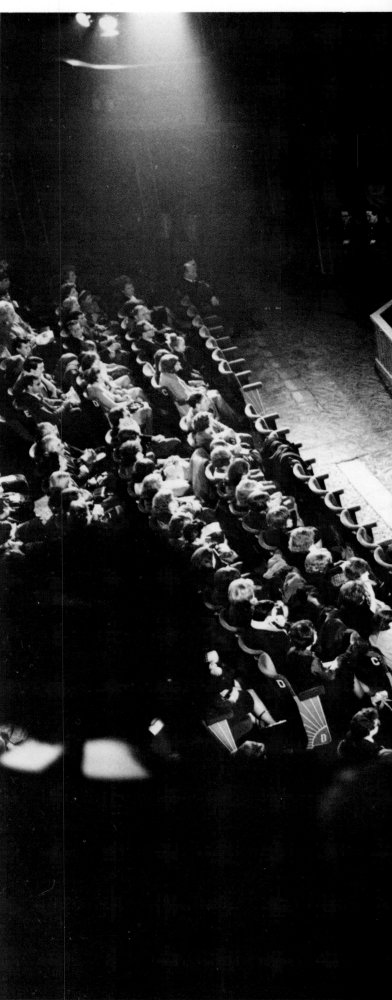

"Juke Box Jury" from the Moss
Empire, Liverpool,
11 December 1963:
*'They really scored here, and set
the precedent for other bands,
like the Stones, to do "Juke Box
Jury" later. They really were
marvellous entertainers, they
could make fun out of anything
and the kids went stark raving
mad! After the show, they played
a few numbers.'*

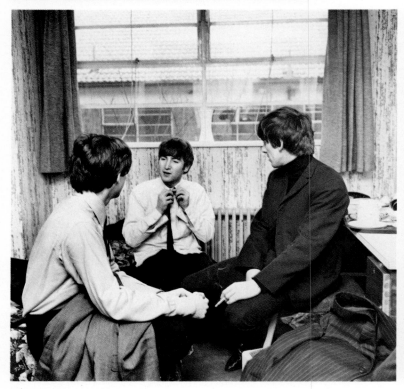

At Elstree, recording "The Morecambe And Wise Show" for ATV, 2 December, 1963:
'It was easy for them to get shows like Top Of The Pops, but they needed to get on the adult viewing schedules. So the Morecambe And Wise Show was perfect. They did just two numbers.'

'Neil fell asleep in the dressing room and Mal Evans watched critically while they rehearsed.'

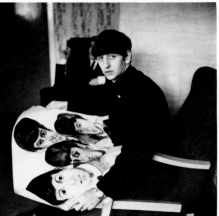

'A present from a fan — they kept as much of all that stuff as they could.'

THE BEATLES FAN CLUB CONCERT,
WIMBLEDON PALAIS,
14 DECEMBER 1963:
*'A concert strictly for fan club
members, and 3000 turned up
from all over the country. It was
probably the best Beatles concert
I ever witnessed and I was
frustrated at not being able to
capture the atmosphere without
a flash. Only two albums had
been released then, but the
merchandising stall sold out
within minutes.'*

'Either side of The Beatles, Neil Aspinall and Bryan Sommerville, their Press Officer, kept the crowd in check.'

'They sat behind the bar, which was of course closed, and greeted every single fan individually.'

'It was the first time they used crowd barriers, but Neil ordered them because the boys would have been torn to pieces. The noise was just incredible.'

THE EMI CHRISTMAS PARTY, ABBEY ROAD, DECEMBER, 1963:
'Abbey Road Studio Number One was converted into a reception area and all the EMI artists, entourages, managers, and so on would gather. The Beatles hated these parties but went to meet people they'd wanted to meet for a long time, like Helen Shapiro, Alma Cogan, and other stars of the time.'

'Gerry Marsden, George Martin and George Harrison.'

THE BEATLES CHRISTMAS SHOW,
FINSBURY PARK ASTORIA,
24 DECEMBER, 1963, 11 JANUARY,
1964:
*'Once again they couldn't hear
their music at all for the noise
of the fans. But they enjoyed
dressing up and acting for the
kids.'*

ABBEY ROAD, DECEMBER 1963:
*'Paul would often shadow
George Martin to learn about
the technicalities of recording.
Here he sat in on Billy J.
Kramer's studio time as he
recorded the follow-up to "Do
You Wanna Know A Secret".'*

BBC Paris Cinema:
'We walked to Cecil Gee's clothes shop in Shaftesbury Avenue from my studio. Whenever we had a bit of time to spare, we'd do some pictures.'

Backstage during Sunday Night At The London Palladium, January, 1964:
'They now had the star dressing room.'

PARIS/ORLY AIRPORT,
14-16 JANUARY, 1964:
'Ringo missed the plane to
Paris, but arrived the next day.
There were posters all over
Paris displaying the pictures
Astrid Kirchherr had taken in
Hamburg.'

'They tasted crepes suzettes for the first time and this waiter did nothing else all day but make crepes for them.'

'They stayed at the George V Hotel in Paris and posed outside, Paul in his Parisian oilskin coat, with which he started a whole fashion craze.'

'Paris Match decided they wanted a big photofeature, including the cover, to be done all in one morning. The Beatles never usually woke up until the afternoon and I was given the unfortunate job of waking them at 9.30am to do the session. I decided it would be a good idea for all concerned if we had a sequence of photos showing them shaving, dressing etc. I insisted they cancel a scheduled New Musical Express interview because Paris Match was more important, and since John had never heard of it he didn't forgive me for months.'

'They did a walkabout down the
Champs Elysees and it was soon
obvious that they couldn't stop
and have a quiet drink.'

'This was a marvellous day. We were eating in a café with the Parisian *Melody Maker* correspondent, Mike Hennessey, when I was summoned back to the hotel by Epstein. I took Mike with me and Epstein broke the news that The Beatles had at last cracked the American market — "I Wanna Hold Your Hand" was Number One on the Cashbox chart. This meant it was more than likely they'd be asked to do the Ed Sullivan Show, since they'd been on the shortlist for a while. The stars and stripes portrait was the first picture I took after the news, to commemorate Stateside success.'

'They had an Austin Princess
imported from England to travel
from the hotel to the Olympia
in, for the concert.'

'Backstage and onstage at the
Olympia. The Beatles were
disappointed with the French in
many ways. Firstly because the
audience was 95% male,
(French parents were strict with
their daughters and believed
The Beatles to be hooligans).
Also, merchandise sales proved
that Ringo was by far the most
popular Beatle in France. All
his pictures would sell out way
ahead of the others and his
name would be shouted
everywhere they went. This
caused a little tension within the
group because, after all, Ringo
was still a session man then. He
wasn't yet a fully fledged
Beatle.'

'Ringo the ever-aspiring photographer.'

'Ringo with my camera in his dressing room, teaching Olympia co-star Sylvie Vartan, how to take a picture.'

'Impromptu interview — they were almost kidnapped off the street and taken into the studios of Europe 1, France's international radio station. It turned out to be one of their best-ever interviews. The interviewer couldn't speak English. The Beatles couldn't speak French. They just talked.'

Leaving Heathrow for America,
7 February, 1964:
*'John and Cynthia had only
recently got married, so she
came too.'*

'Dick James (with the glasses),
The Beatles music publisher,
bids farewell to his boys, along
with lawyer David Jacobs, while
Epstein looks on.'

'The pre-flight press conference.
Maureen Cleave of the Evening
Standard was determined to be
photographed with them.'

ARRIVING AT KENNEDY AIRPORT, THE ED SULLIVAN SHOW, CBS, NEW YORK, FEBRUARY, 1964:
'Paul's bemused expression tells the story. Circling over Kennedy airport, we could see an astronomical crowd of people. There'd never been crowds like that before — we honestly thought the President was due to arrive. In front of Paul is Phil Spector, who travelled with us though he did very little with The Beatles.'

'Contrary to popular opinion, pop stars were given a rigorous going-over at customs.'

'The crowd outside the Plaza
Hotel, New York. The girls
were wearing T-shirts (bearing
my design) supplied them by
Seltaeb, the merchandising
company set up for the
American tour. Each fan was
given a free T-shirt, one dollar
and a bus ride to the airport.
And that's really how
Beatlemania started in
America.'

'With Bryan Sommerville in the Plaza Hotel. The Maysle brothers were filming and Ringo looks unusually disconcerted. They had a whole floor reserved at the hotel, including a mail room for the sacks of fan mail that arrived from England every day.'

'The Ed Sullivan show consisted of all British stars that day.'

'The Ed Sullivan show. George was very poorly and stayed at the hotel with his sister looking after him, so they had to use Neil Aspinall for rehearsals.'

*'The local press went crazy on
stage with them and they
insisted Brian Epstein was
photographed with them.'*

NEW YORK CARNEGIE HALL
CONCERTS 7 FEBRUARY, 1964:
*'The queue for the Carnegie
Hall concert was enormous. The
anti-Beatle protesters, who
manifested themselves especially
in Detroit, were there too.'*

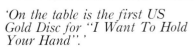

PRESS RECEPTION IN THE NEW YORK PLAZA:

'With Bryan Sommerville conducting the press conference, they weren't at all nervous, even though it was coast to coast press. Just like they conquered me, they conquered the whole of the United States. George Martin had been worried seeing the barrage of microphones, photographers and television cameras. But they used their style, sincerity, looks, and won everybody over.'

'On the table is the first US Gold Disc for "I Want To Hold Your Hand".'

'Filming with the Maysles brothers in the Plaza. Brian Epstein allowed them to film on the Washington trip next day, which eventually became a full-length film.'

'They had to have mounted police escorting their car through the crowds. I regret that there were no wide-angle lenses in those days.'

'They managed a walk in Central Park.'

'Paul posing for me with
George's sister, who lived in
America and joined us there.'

'We woke up the morning we
were supposed to fly to
Washington knee-deep in snow.
The Beatles had heard things
about American airlines and
refused to fly, demanding a
train. They coupled a carriage
on to the regular Washington
train and we got there on time.'

'They were very glad to have gone by train. They saw a little of snow-covered America.'

'I left Ringo with one of my cameras. He was the only good photographer in The Beatles. He also shot with the Maysles' movie camera.'

'Ringo made a real friend with the attendant. George spontaneously grabbed his hat and tray. Nothing was ever posed, it was all ad lib and I just had to anticipate each time.

'The Beatles are greeted at Washington station, with a banner from WWDC, Washington's local radio station.'

BEFORE AND DURING THE CONCERT
AT WASHINGTON COLISEUM,
11 FEBRUARY, 1964:
*'They threw millions of jelly
babies on stage after Paul's
comment that he liked them.'*

*'Ringo was on a revolving
platform, so all the audience
had a chance to see him. It took
half an hour for him to recover
from his dizziness.'*

*'They gave a press conference
from the stage before the show
to the international press corps.'*

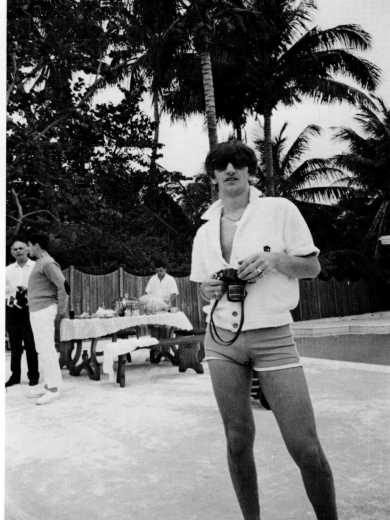

MIAMI, 13-22 FEBRUARY, 1964:
*'Miami was a remarkable
experience. We had a whole
floor in the Hotel Deauville, and
we also borrowed a villa off a
millionaire. They enjoyed it so
much, you can see in the
pictures there's not one
miserable face. It was as if
they'd been born into it, they
were so nonchalant.'*

'A good review in a local paper.'   'They hated rehearsals in Miami and just walked in out of the pool.'   'A famous picture of a famous picture being taken. This shot was eventually used on the cover of Life magazine. They couldn't believe that photographer was using flash in the middle of the day.'

'Berry Gordy of Tamla Motown came down and the boys insisted on being photographed with him. Yet another souvenir.'

'Some girls came autograph hunting in the sea and of course The Beatles wanted something else from them. It made them laugh though!'

'I knew that lose or win (with Sonnie Liston) Cassius Clay would be a star, so we went to his gym in Miami. He was marvellous considering he had no idea who The Beatles were. But his manager had heard of them and when he found out they came from England, he did whatever they wanted. I only wish I'd had a movie camera, to film their simulated fights.'

'The hairdressing salon of the Hotel Deauville, where Sonnie Liston's wife worked.'

'Everywhere people were Beatle-crazy. Even at the gas stations in Miami they were wearing Beatle wigs.'

'The second Ed Sullivan appearance, live from Miami. They just never got tired, for them this wasn't work, it was enjoyment.'

Returning from US Kennedy
Airport to London Heathrow,
22 February, 1964:

'The Heathrow airport
authorities decided to investigate
how so many people got on to
the tarmac. They used these
pictures as testimony and I
believe there were a few sackings
as a result.'

TWICKENHAM, MARCH 1964:
FILMING "A HARD DAY'S NIGHT":
*'The whole Ready Steady Go
stage was reconstructed for the
film sequence and The Beatles
were made to dress in clothes
they never normally wore.'*

*'She was an extra, but the
picture captures perfectly the
twinkle in John's eye, that was
so typical of him. It was here
that John and I had an
argument which meant I saw
less and less of them. He began
not to trust anybody, believing
they were being fleeced by
everybody. And because he was
taking drugs, his paranoia was
worsened. That day, he actually
accused me of making a fortune
out of The Beatles, while they
saw nothing.'*

'Paul half-heartedly hides from the camera with Jane Asher.'

'Julie Andrews and Dick Van Dyke were filming "Mary Poppins" at the same studios.'

'A trailer for "A Hard Day's Night", serious faces on a ridiculous set.'

YOU MAY TELEPHONE FROM HERE

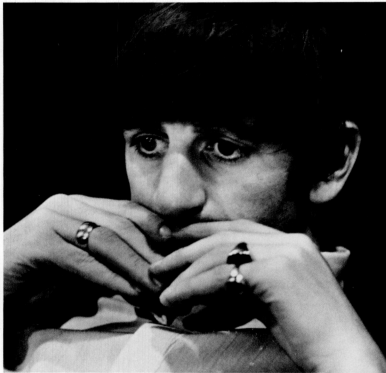

ABBEY ROAD, FEBRUARY, MARCH, APRIL, 1964: RECORDING "A HARD DAY'S NIGHT":
'And so Ringo started the ring fashion...'

"AROUND THE BEATLES". ATV
WEMBLEY, 6 MAY, 1964:

OUTSIDE THE NATIONAL PORTRAIT
GALLERY, LONDON. MAY, 1964:
*'I happened to spot these as I
walked past. Later, I would look
at John's face next to Kennedy's
and feel it was more than
coincidental.'*

London Palladium, 'Night Of 100
Stars', 23 July, 1964:
*'They were impressed by
Laurence Olivier, but John was
keen to speak to me as this was
the first time we'd met since the
argument.'*

OPERA HOUSE, BLACKPOOL,
26 JULY, 1964:
'Yet another 'Beatle-iner.'

*'One of Paul's favourite poses, I
have so many pictures like this.'*

THE BEATLES CHRISTMAS SHOW,
HAMMERSMITH ODEON, LONDON
24 DECEMBER, 1964 -
16 JANUARY 1965:
'The back row consists of
Fourmost members, Dakotas
and Barron Knights. Centre
row: Fourmost member, Tommy
Quickly, Billy J. Kramer, Rolf
Harris, Cilla Black, Fourmost
member. The Beatles in front.'

'After the photocall comedian
Rolf Harris demonstrated his
strength on a cardboard Ringo.
They enjoyed Christmas Shows
because they were family
occasions, and during the couple
of years they had existed there
had been scarcely one boy at
their live shows. So the
Christmas Shows were a
pleasant change.'

ABBEY ROAD, FEBRUARY-MARCH, 1965. RECORDING "HELP":
John's Triumph Herald car.

'John is smiling right at me but you could never tell — like a dog who has rabies, you never knew when he would jump and bite.'

FILMING "HELP" AT TWICKENHAM
STUDIOS, FEBRUARY-APRIL, 1965:
*'Director Dick Lester stays
solemn in the background.'*

*'No press, no photos. They were
under terrible strain while they
were filming.'*

*'Paul with his younger brother
Mike McGear in the yard at
Twickenham studios solving a
family problem.'*

'John allowed Chris Denning of Radio Luxembourg to interview him briefly.'

THE ROYAL VARIETY CLUB LUNCH,
JUNE, 1965:
*'Paul was the only Beatle there
and was pleased they'd seated
him next to David Frost.'*

THE MBE PRESS CONFERENCE AT
THE SAVILLE THEATRE,
26 OCTOBER, 1965:
*'Witty repartee soon turned sour
when other recipients returned
their honours as protest against
The Beatles, and John
eventually returned his too,
although he regretted it.'*

BBC PLAYHOUSE THEATRE,
CHARING CROSS, LONDON:
'With Brian Matthew before the
performance. They became
easier and easier to work with.
They knew me so well I just had
to raise a finger or an eyebrow
and they'd know what I wanted,
I never had to shout.'

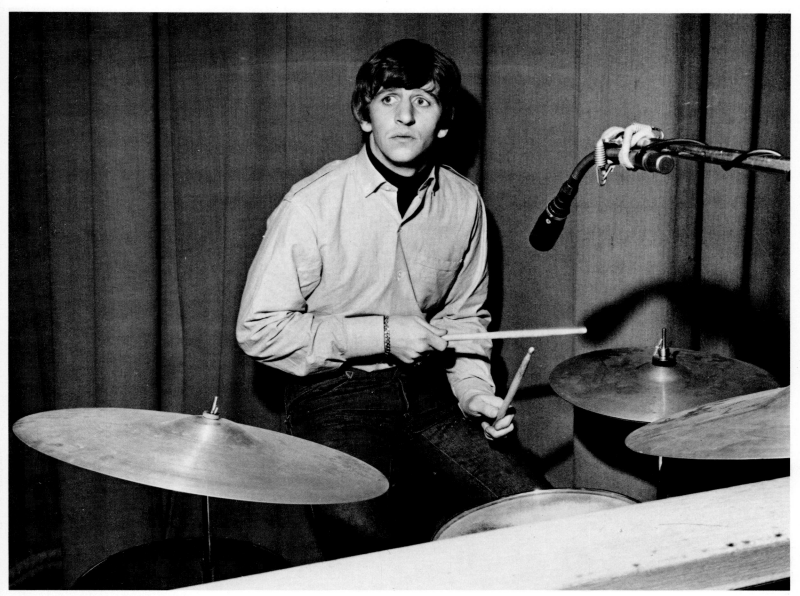

JULY 2, 1964:
THE BEATLES ARRIVE BACK IN
BRITAIN AFTER THEIR TOUR OF
THE FAR EAST, AUSTRALIA AND
NEW ZEALAND.
(OPPOSITE PAGE) LEAVING THE
PLANE WHILE DEREK TAYLOR
(RIGHT) THEIR PRESS OFFICER
LOOKS ON.

AUSTRALIAN APPLES PROMOTION
ADVERTISEMENT, APRIL, 1965: